TOOLS OF WAR

WEAPONS
and VEHICLES

of the
VIETNAM WAR

by Elizabeth Summers

Reading Consultant:
Barbara J. Fox
Professor Emerita
North Carolina State University

CAPSTONE PRESS
a capstone imprint

Blazers Books are published by Capstone Press,
1710 Roe Crest Drive, North Mankato, Minnesota 56003.
www.capstonepub.com

Library of Congress Cataloging-in-Publication Data
Summers, Elizabeth.
Weapons and vehicles of the Vietnam War / by Elizabeth Summers.
        pages cm.—(Blazers books. Tools of war.)
Includes bibliographical references and index.
Summary: "Describes various weapons and vehicles used by U.S. and North Vietnamese forces during
the Vietnam War"—Provided by publisher.
ISBN 978-1-4914-4082-7 (library binding)
ISBN 978-1-4914-4116-9 (ebook pdf)
1. Vietnam War, 1961-1975—Equipment and supplies—Juvenile literature. 2. Vehicles, Military—
History—20th century—Juvenile literature. 3. Vietnam War, 1961-1975—Transportation—Juvenile
literature. I. Title.
 DS559.8.S9S86 2016
 959.704'3—dc23   2015006160

Editorial Credits
Anna Butzer, editor; Heidi Thompson, designer; Jo Miller, media researcher;
Katy LaVigne, production specialist

Photo Credits
Alamy: Avpics, cover, Military Images, 10, Mim Friday, 15, RIA Novosti, 26; Corbis: Bettmann, 12-13,
18, 28-29, Bettmann/Dennis Cook, 16-17, Bettmann/Shunsuke Akatsuka, 17 (inset), Science Faction/
William James Warren, 5, Tim Page, 22-23; Getty Images: Popperfoto/Paul Popper, 19; Newscom:
akg-images, 6-7, 9; Shutterstock: Jackson Gee, 11; Wikimedia: NARA/Department of Defense, 29
(inset), U.S. Army Military History Institute/AHEC, 21, U.S. Army Heritage and Education Center,
24-25, U.S. Navy National Museum of Naval Aviation, 27

Design Elements:
Shutterstock: angelinast, aodaodaodaod, artjazz, Brocreative, ilolab, kasha_malasha, Peter Sobolev

Printed in the United States of America in North Mankato, Minnesota.
052015   008823CGF15

TABLE OF CONTENTS

IN THE JUNGLE

In 1954 Vietnam split into North and South Vietnam. By 1959 the two countries were at war. North Vietnam wanted **communism**, but South Vietnam did not. The Soviet Union and China supported North Vietnam. The United States supported South Vietnam.

communism—a form of government in which the land, homes, and businesses belong to the government

UH-1B helicopters

The United States had one of the strongest military forces in the world. They expected to defeat the North Vietnamese and the South **Viet Cong** rebels quickly. Instead, the Vietnam War dragged on until 1975. It was one of the deadliest and most expensive wars in history.

Viet Cong—rebels who fought against the government of South Vietnam

WEAPONS

Rifles and Shotguns

Soldiers on both sides used lightweight guns, such as rifles and **shotguns**. The North Vietnamese used many old guns given to them by the Soviet Union and China. North Vietnamese soldiers mainly used AK-47 rifles. The Viet Cong often made their own weapons.

FACT
The Viet Cong used bike parts and pieces of old guns to make rifles. They used water pipes to make shotguns.

shotgun–a firearm used to fire small shots at short range
range–the longest distance at which a weapon can still hit its target

M16 Rifle

	AK-47 Rifle	M16 Rifle
Country	North Vietnam	United States
Firing Range	1,148 feet (350 m)	1,509 feet (460 m)
Weight	7.7 pounds (3.5 kg)	7 pounds (3.2 kg)

U.S. soldiers often used the M16 rifle and the 12-gauge shotgun to fight enemies up close. The wide blast range of the 12-gauge shotgun was useful during Viet Cong **raids**.

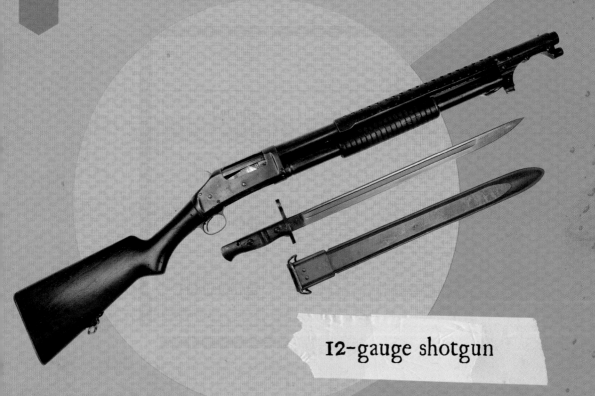

12-gauge shotgun

raid—a sudden, surprise attack

FACT

The United States had been preparing for a war
with the Soviet Union. They made new and improved
weapons. These weapons were used in Vietnam instead.

AK-47 rifle

Flamethrowers and Explosives

U.S. soldiers used flamethrowers to
search and clear secret underground
tunnels. They also set trees and dry plants
on fire to force enemies to retreat.

Both the United States and North Vietnamese armies used small explosives such as **grenades**. The U.S dropped or launched millions of **cluster bombs**. The Viet Cong buried thousands of **land mines**.

Fact

The Viet Cong used grenades in booby traps. Grenades were attached to trip wires and would explode when triggered.

grenade—a small bomb that can be thrown or launched
cluster bomb—a bomb that holds several "mini-bombs" the size of tennis balls
land mine—an explosive device buried underground that explodes when stepped on

stick grenades

pineapple grenades

	U.S Pineapple Grenade	German Stick Grenade
Weight	1.3 pounds (0.59 kg)	1.3 pounds (0.59 kg)
Time Before Explosion	4 seconds	4 seconds

Artillery

Both sides used heavy weapons and **artillery** to support troops in battle. These powerful weapons destroyed enemy artillery and vehicles. The U.S. military used the 105 mm **howitzer**.

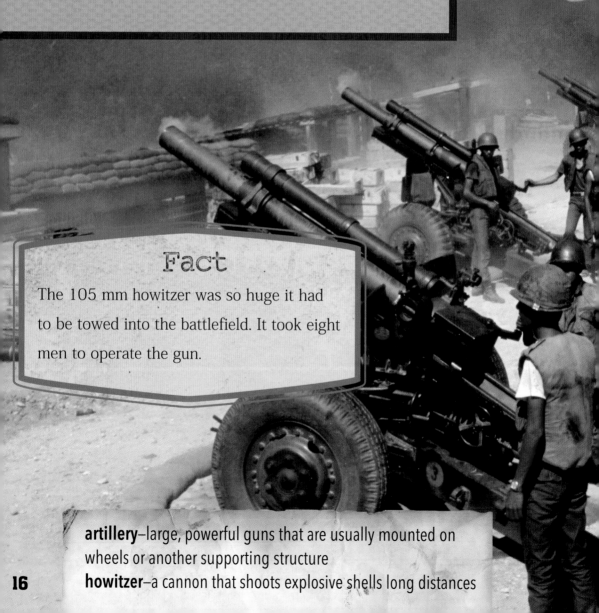

Fact

The 105 mm howitzer was so huge it had to be towed into the battlefield. It took eight men to operate the gun.

artillery—large, powerful guns that are usually mounted on wheels or another supporting structure

howitzer—a cannon that shoots explosive shells long distances

	U.S. M19 60 mm Mortar	U.S. 90 mm M67 Recoilless Rifle	U.S. 105 mm howitzer	Soviet M46 130 mm Field Gun
Weight	52 pounds (23.6 kg)	37.5 pounds (17 kg)	3,298 pounds (1,496 kg)	16,975 pounds (7,700 kg)
Firing Range	1.1 miles (1.8 km)	1.3 miles (2.1 km)	7.1 miles (11.4 km)	17 miles (27.4 km)

helicopter carrying howitzer

North Vietnamese fighters used
Soviet antiaircraft missiles to destroy
many U.S. planes and helicopters.
Each missile used a **heat-seeking
guidance system** and carried
a 2.5-pound (1.1 kg) **warhead.**

M19 60 mm mortar

antiaircraft gun

Fact

The M19 60 mm mortar could be carried by a single U.S. soldier. It shot up to 30 explosives per minute.

heat-seeking guidance system–a guidance system that points a missile toward targets that give off infrared radiation
warhead–the part of a missile that contains the explosive

VEHICLES

Armored Vehicles

The U.S. and North Vietnamese forces used armored vehicles such as tanks. But heavy tanks often got stuck in the mud.

	U.S. M48 Tank	M-113 Armored Personnel Carrier	BMP-1 Armored Personnel Carrier
Weight	49.6 tons (45 mt)	13.6 tons (12 mt)	14.6 tons (13 mt)
Speed	30 miles per hour (48 km/hour)	40 miles per hour (64 km/hour)	40 miles per hour (64 km/hour)
Weapons Carried	2 machine guns	machine gun; sometimes served as an antiaircraft and flamethrower vehicle	semi-automatic gun, missile launcher

M48 tank

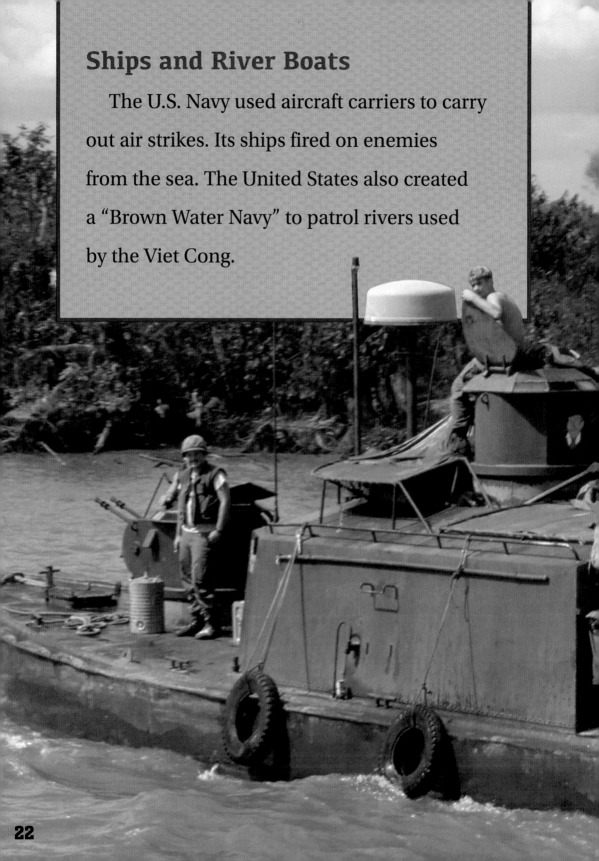

Ships and River Boats

The U.S. Navy used aircraft carriers to carry out air strikes. Its ships fired on enemies from the sea. The United States also created a "Brown Water Navy" to patrol rivers used by the Viet Cong.

Fact

North Vietnamese troops used small boats called "**junks**." They were used to sneak weapons and supplies to troops on the rivers.

junk–a Chinese sailing boat with square sails and a flat bottom

Helicopters and Planes

Helicopters were widely used by the United States for the first time in the Vietnam War. Unlike airplanes, helicopters could land in small clearings to drop off and pick up soldiers.

UH-1D helicopter

FACT

The Bell UH-1 was nicknamed "Huey." It was used to pick up wounded soldiers and to drop off troops for surprise attacks.

Fighter and bomber planes played important roles in the Vietnam War. The Soviet MiG-21 helped the North Vietnamese wreck U.S. bombing missions. But U.S. forces had the faster F4 Phantom II.

MiG-21 airplanes

F4 Phantom II bomber plane

FACT

The F4 Phantom II carried many
weapons, such as radar-guided bombs.

Vietnam's thick jungle gave the Viet Cong cover. So U.S. forces used planes to drop deadly chemicals on enemy positions. People who came into contact with these chemicals died or became sick. The Vietnam War caused great and lasting damage to both sides.

napalm–a sticky chemical substance that burns hotter than 2,000 degrees Fahrenheit (1,093 degrees Celsius)

Fact

The United States used a chemical called **napalm** to harm the enemy. U.S. forces also used chemicals to kill the leaves off trees and plants.

GLOSSARY

artillery (ar-TIL-uh-ree)—large, powerful guns that are usually mounted on wheels or another supporting structure

cluster bomb (KLUHS-tur BAHM)—a bomb that holds several "mini-bombs" the size of tennis balls

communism (KAHM-yuh-ni-zuhm)—a form of government in which the land, homes, and businesses belong to the government

grenade (gruh-NAYD)—a small bomb that can be thrown or launched

heat-seeking guidance system (HEET-seek-ing GAHYD-ns SISS-tuhm)—a guidance system that points a missile toward targets that give off infrared radiation

howitzer (HOU-uht-sur)—a cannon that shoots explosive shells long distances

junk (JUHNGK)—a Chinese sailing boat with square sails and a flat bottom

land mine (LAND MINE)—an explosive device buried underground that explodes when stepped on

napalm (NEY-pahm)—a sticky chemical substance that burns hotter than 2,000 degree Fahrenheit (1,093 degrees Celsius)

raid (RAYD)—a sudden, surprise attack

range (RAYNJ)—the longest distance at which a weapon can still hit its target

shotgun (SHOT-guhn)—a firearm used to fire small shots at short range

Viet Cong (VEE-et KOHNG)—rebels who fought against the government of South Vietnam

warhead (WOR-hed)—the part of a missile that contains the explosive

READ MORE

Cooke, Tim. *The Vietnam War on the Front Lines*. Life on the Front Lines. North Mankato, Minn.: Capstone Pub., 2015.

Samuels, Charlie. *Machines and Weaponry of the Vietnam War*. Machines That Won the War. New York: Gareth Stevens Pub., 2013.

INTERNET SITES

FactHound offers a safe, fun way to find Internet sites related to this book. All of the sites on FactHound have been researched by our staff

Here's all you do:

Visit *www.facthound.com*

Type in this code: 9781491440827

Check out projects, games and lots more at
www.capstonekids.com

INDEX